L.

7 Oct. 1914

Virginia

LEONARD WOOLF

CLIVE BELL

VITA SACKVILLE-WEST

VANESSA BELL

LYTTON STRACHEY

E. M. FORSTER

RUPERT BROOKE

 Woolf AND HER CIRCLE

FRANCIS O. MATTSON

Henry W. and Albert A.
Berg Collection of English and
American Literature

The New York Public Library
1993

Published for the exhibition
Virginia Woolf and Her Circle,
Berg Exhibition Room,
The New York Public Library,
October 15, 1993–April 9, 1994

This publication was produced
with the generous assistance of
Leonard L. Milberg.

For permission to reproduce illustrations
and to quote Virginia Woolf, Vanessa Bell,
and other members of the Stephen and
Bell families, we are grateful to Quentin
Bell.

ISBN 0-87104-434-X

*The photograph of Virginia Woolf
reproduced on the cover was taken by
George Charles Beresford in 1902.
It is part of an album of photographs
kept by Violet Dickinson. The back-
ground is the first page of the holograph of* To the Lighthouse, *which is
reproduced in full on page 50.*

*Leonard Woolf's inscription to his wife
in a copy of his novel* The Wise Virgins
is reproduced on the half-title page.

CONTENTS

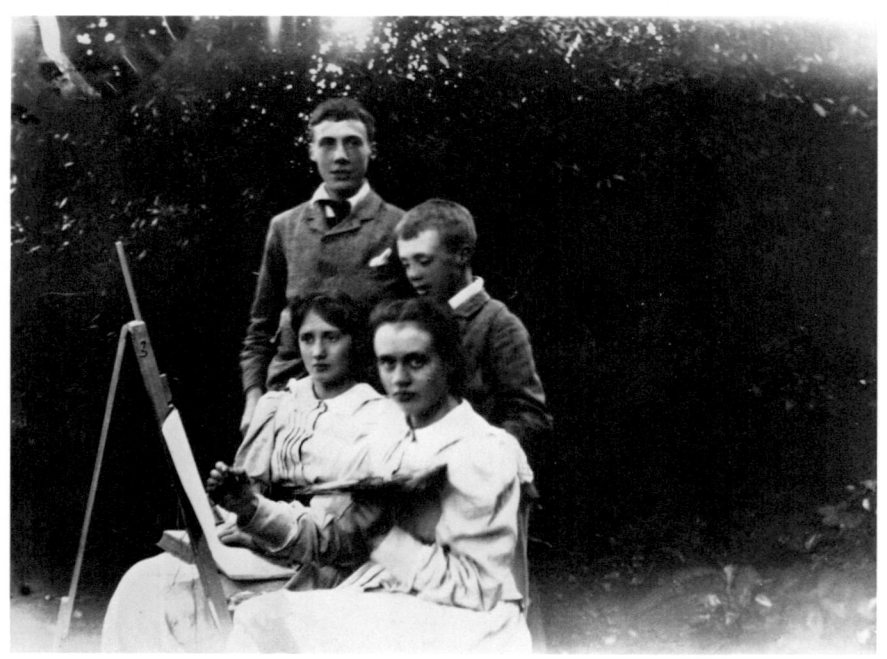

Vanessa Stephen (at easel)
and (clockwise) Virginia,
Thoby, and Adrian Stephen
(item 6)

Virginia Woolf is distinguished as a writer for her novels, short stories, critical essays, diaries, and letters and, in the history of fiction, for her innovations in technique. She is the central figure in the Bloomsbury Group, so prominent in the literary and artistic scene in post–World War I Britain.

Virginia Woolf was born Adeline Virginia Stephen in London on January 25, 1882, the third child of Leslie Stephen and Julia Jackson. Her parents had each been married before and had children from their previous marriages. Stephen's first wife was Harriet Marian Thackeray, the younger of the novelist's two daughters, and they had one child, Laura. Julia Jackson's previous marriage was to Herbert Duckworth, and their three children were George, Stella, and Gerald. In addition to Virginia, the children of Leslie and Julia Stephen were Vanessa (1879–1961), Thoby (1880–1906), and Adrian (1883–1948).

Leslie Stephen was a distinguished man of letters and a philosopher, editor of the *Cornhill Magazine* and of the massive undertaking that was the *Dictionary of National Biography*. His family was part of the intellectual elite of Britain, which included such other families as the Stracheys, the Macaulays, and the Trevelyans. Virginia, unlike her brothers, was educated at home under her father's guidance and with free run of his library. In 1904 she became a professional author with the publication of her first essay (on a visit to the Brontës' home at Haworth).

Virginia, whose mental health was fragile, suffered her first breakdown after her mother's death in 1895; her second after her father's death in 1904; and her third in 1913, a year after her marriage to Leonard Woolf and before the publication of her first novel. Thereafter, the imminent appearance of a new work would be cause for concern about Virginia's health. It was her fear of another breakdown that led to her suicide in 1941.

Bloomsbury, with which Virginia is inextricably associated, is a place, a group, and a state of mind. According to Quentin Bell, Virginia's nephew and biographer, the Bloomsbury Group had its beginning among a group of undergraduates at Trinity College, Cambridge, in the fall of 1899. This nuclear group consisted of some of the members of the exclusive "Apostles" – Leonard Woolf, Lytton Strachey, Saxon Sydney-Turner – plus Thoby Stephen and Clive Bell. After the death of Leslie Stephen, his children abandoned their home in fashionable Kensington for Bloomsbury, where, following Thoby Stephen's graduation from Cambridge, his friends began meeting at the Stephens' Thursday evening "at homes" in Gordon Square. Bloomsbury was avant-garde in art and modernist in literature, but the emphasis of the exhibition and this checklist, given the nature of the Berg Collection, is necessarily on the literary.

Many of the important figures represented here were part of Virginia Woolf's circle, but not of Bloomsbury. The aristocratic Vita Sackville-West and Lady Ottoline Morrell were not Bloomsbury; E. M. Forster is marginally Blooms-bury; Rupert Brooke, who went "skinny-dipping" with Virginia, detested much of what Bloomsbury represented.

Virginia Woolf may have been a central figure in Bloomsbury, but there was nothing parochial about her work
or her achievement. It is the aim of this checklist to outline
her writing career and the context in which she wrote.
The arrangement is essentially chronological. In the anno-
tations we have followed the practice of Quentin Bell in his
biography of his aunt and referred to "Virginia Stephen"
for the period before her marriage and "Virginia Woolf"
after.

This exhibition on Virginia Woolf and her circle was
prompted by no anniversary: it happily coincided, however, with the completion of a project to microfilm the
entire Virginia Woolf archive in the Berg Collection, both
for preservation purposes and to make the manuscripts
more widely available. Now that the original manuscripts
may enjoy a rest, it seems a good time to share one of
our most popular research collections with an equally
interested larger public.

Wolf's-head logo of the
Hogarth Press, a pun
on the proprietors' surname,
designed by Vanessa Bell

The Stephen family, in a photograph taken ca. 1890–95. Back row, left to right: Gerald Duckworth, Virginia, Thoby, and Vanessa Stephen, and George Duckworth; front row: Adrian, Julia Prinsep Jackson, and Sir Leslie Stephen (item 6)

1   Julia Margaret Cameron. Portrait photograph of Julia
     Prinsep Jackson Stephen, 1867. Gift of Hamill and Barker
     in memory of Dr. John D. Gordan.

This photograph of the second Mrs. Leslie Stephen
was taken in 1867, before her first marriage to Herbert
Duckworth, by her aunt Julia Margaret Cameron.

2   Stella Duckworth Hills. Letter to her mother, Julia Prinsep
     Jackson Stephen, [1882].

Virginia Stephen was born January 25, 1882. In this letter
Stella mentions her still unnamed half sister, referring to her
as "Beauty."

*. . . I hope that you have had a good night, & that you
are better & that all the Babies are quite well. I wonder
what you will call "Beauty," I can't think of any name
for her, have you had her weighed yet. Please give all the
Babies lots of kisses for me. . . .*

3   Leslie Stephen. "Science of Ethics." Holograph manuscript,
     [1882].

A distinguished man of letters, editor of the *Cornhill
Magazine* and the *Dictionary of National Biography*, and
a philosopher, Stephen published his *Science of Ethics*
in 1882. It "summed up, in the light of his study of Mill,
Darwin, and Herbert Spencer, his final conclusions on
the dominant problems of life" (*DNB*). This concern with

ethics carried over to the next generation, which, however, took G. E. Moore's *Principia Ethica* as its guide.

Hugh Walpole has noted on the flyleaf of the first volume of the manuscript: "Virginia Woolf, requested by me, got her brother [Adrian] to give this to the Red Cross Sale where I bought it July 1940. She is of course Leslie Stephen's daughter."

4   Leslie Stephen. Letter to his wife Julia Prinsep Jackson Stephen, April 17, 1887.

This letter to Mrs. Stephen concludes with a glimpse of five-year-old Virginia:

Ginia said she would make a speech tonight. She stood in the window & declaimed a long rigmarole about a crow & a book till her hearers coughed her down. She would have gone on till now.

Your old L.S.

5   James Russell Lowell. Letter, signed Godpapa, to Virginia Stephen, Aug. 22, 1888.

This is Lowell's reply to the "earliest [surviving] document in [Virginia's] hand" (Quentin Bell), a letter written at age six to her godfather, James Russell Lowell, the American poet then serving as U.S. minister to England.

6   Stella Duckworth Hills. An album of family photographs kept by Stella Duckworth (Mrs. Jack Hills), Virginia's half sister, who died in 1897. The photographs were taken about the time represented in the first section of *To the Lighthouse*.

7   Virginia Stephen. Diary, June 1897. Holograph.

Several weeks before her fifteenth birthday, Virginia began

her first diary, recording the minutiae of daily life as well as comments on her writing and on literature. Of the six early journals, 1897–1909 (published in 1990 under the title *A Passionate Apprentice*), only the first was a true diary; the others were largely literary exercises.

8   **George Charles Beresford. Portrait photographs of Virginia Stephen and Sir Leslie and Virginia Stephen, 1902, mounted in an album kept by Violet Dickinson.**

9   **Virginia Stephen. Letter to Violet Dickinson, [Feb. 21, 1904].**

Dickinson was a friend of Stella Duckworth's and became a lifelong friend of Virginia's. This letter was written the evening Leslie Stephen died.

My Violet,

Father has been becoming less conscious all the afternoon & evening. He now does not know us. Wilson says the poison must have reached the kidneys, & he does not think it possible for him to get any better. He says he may die tonight. It is 11.30 now, & he comes again later, so I will add anything. Father was very restless, talking to himself, but Wilson has given him morphia so that he now lies quite quietly.

11.30. Wilson [has] just been. He says there is no change, and thinks he will probably get through the night. They give him morphia if he is at all restless, so he has no pain, & simply lies without moving most of the time. I will telegraph tomorrow morning. We are sending for Adrian.

Dont come, my Violet. Stay quiet, & get well. There is nothing to be done. I have been sitting with him – so have we all. It is quite peaceful. He doesn't take any notice. He seemed a little better this morning, & saw Kitty & talked away: it came on quite suddenly at 2.

Yr. AVS.

10   Frederic William Maitland. *The Life and Letters of Leslie Stephen*. London: Duckworth, 1906.

The first biography of Leslie Stephen appeared two years after his death and includes Virginia's earliest appearance in book form. On pages 474–76, under the semi-anonymity of "one of his daughters," she recorded impressions of her father.

11   Photograph of Violet Dickinson, in an album of photographs covering the period 1895–1906. With a companion photograph of "OED," her brother Oswald.

12   Virginia Stephen. Letter to Violet Dickinson, Sept. 26, [1904].

Virginia suffered her first breakdown after her mother's death in 1895 and a second after her father's death. She spent some time at Violet Dickinson's house, where she attempted to kill herself. By the end of the summer, she was recovering from the episode of madness and staying with her family. In a letter to Dickinson at the end of September, Virginia reflects on the experience:

. . . Oh my Violet, if there were a God I should bless him for having delivered me safe & sound from the miseries of the last six months! You cant think what an exquisite joy every minute of my life is to me now, & my only prayer is that I may live to be 70. I do think I may emerge less selfish & cocksure than I went in & with greater understanding of the troubles of others.

Sorrow, such as I feel now for Father, is soothing & natural, & makes life more worth having, if sadder. I can never tell you what you have been to me all this time – for one thing you wouldn't believe it – but if affection is worth anything you have, & always will have, mine.

It is queer now that I am better that I feel physically so

much more. I am rather bothered with neuralgia, but that
goes away with food & fresh air, & I hardly attempt to do
more than bask & eat.

It will be nice to see you again. Nessa so happy.

Yr. loving
AVS

I am longing to begin work.

13   Virginia Stephen. "Haworth: November, 1904." Holograph essay.

The year 1904 marked Virginia's debut as a professional
writer. Her first published essay recounts a visit to the
Brontë family home. She had already made an appearance
as a book reviewer in the December 14, 1904, issue of
The Guardian reviewing a novel by William Dean Howells.

14   Photographs of 46 Gordon Square, London, and the Bloomsbury Group plaque at 50 Gordon Square.

At the end of 1904, the Stephen children moved from the
family home at 22 Hyde Park Gate, Kensington, to 46
Gordon Square in Bloomsbury. It was to Gordon Square
that Thoby and Adrian invited their Cambridge friends,
notably Lytton Strachey, Desmond MacCarthy, Saxon
Sydney-Turner, and Clive Bell, and it was here in March
1905 that the first of the Bloomsbury Group's Thursday
evening gatherings occurred. Virginia and Adrian remained
here until Vanessa's marriage in 1907 to Clive Bell.

15   E. M. Forster. *The Longest Journey*. Edinburgh: Blackwood, 1907.

The opening scene of *The Longest Journey*, Forster's
second and his favorite among his novels, is set in turn-of-
the-century Cambridge, at a Saturday evening meeting

Vanessa Stephen's sketch for a never-completed portrait of Lord Robert Cecil, in a letter to her sister, Virginia (item 16)

of the "Apostles." The Cambridge Conversazione Society or "The Society," more familiarly the "Apostles," was an exclusive group of intellectuals, primarily undergraduates. Forster came into association with Bloomsbury through his Apostolic friendships.

16 **Vanessa Stephen. Letter to her sister, Virginia Stephen, [April 17, 1906].**

Addressed to "Beloved Billy," one of Virginia's nicknames (as in Billy Goat), this letter includes a sketch for a not-to-be-completed portrait of Lord Robert Cecil.

. . . I'm afraid it isnt at all a work of genius for I have done very little work as you know from my previous veracious accounts of the manner of spending my day, & then Lord R. never sits. The plan of the work is this

[sketch]

Can you make head or tail of it? He is sitting at his writing table on which are strewn papers, etc. At the right is a red curtain (window sill with bits of sunlight coming through on to the curtain & table. The wall behind him is white. It is quite small. The worst of it is that I'm afraid it isn't very like him. However I hope to get it like tomorrow. I expect its atrociously painted & its not very original! So you see I dont think much of it, & I would give a good deal to do him well. But it cant be helped. I think Nelly [Lady Robert Cecil] quite likes it.

17 **Thoby Stephen. Letter to Leonard Woolf, Oct. 10, 1906.**

Woolf, a college friend of Thoby's, accepted a position in Ceylon after leaving Cambridge, from late 1904 to June 1911. Thoby wrote Woolf from Greece, which he was visiting with his brother and sisters:

My dear Woolf.

Its about time I wrote to you and this seems a good place to do it from. It occurred to me this summer that this year would be the last in wh[ich] I could take a decent holiday as I was called to the bar in June. Consequently Adrian & I started off in August. We came here via Trieste taking a coasting steamer down Dalmatia and putting in 10 days in Montenegro. . . . My sister who came out to meet us here has developed appendicitis, wh[ich] though she is now convalescent may keep us here some time. This country w[oul]d fairly make you sit up. It is by far the finest in the world apart from what's in it – barring its people who are mostly devils. As for the temples etc one can't get a notion of them anywhere else. I shan't go in for a description of it however. I suppose you hear from Turner now & again. Some pretty important operas & symphonies may be ex- pected from him soon. . . . I heard from Bell the other day. The Strache [Lytton Strachey] has been staying with him in Scotland and apparently catching trout. Strache was going on to live in a cottage with Keynes, his brother & young Trinity. I apprehend scandal. The Cingalese con- tagion seems to spread in Cambridge not but what here [?] young fellows are all humbugs. Lamb is staying on at Cambridge for a year. He assumes the God, and finds priests. You have no doubt heard the romance of Harry & Nina from Turner – a sorry business. Well my good fellow a letter from you would be uncommonly pleasant. The difficulty in writing to you at these long intervals is that one has no notion what in particular to say – did you ever give me your opinion of Euphrosyne? Do anyhow.

Yours ever J. T. S.

18   Lytton Strachey. Letter to Leonard Woolf, Nov. 21, 1906.

On his return from Greece, Thoby Stephen ("the Goth") became ill. What was at first thought to be malaria was soon realized to be typhoid fever, from which he died on

November 20. The following day Strachey wrote Woolf with the news:

You must be prepared for something terrible. You will never see the Goth again. He died yesterday. I know no more, except that his pneumonia turned out to be typhoid. . . . I don't understand what crowning pleasure there can be for us without him, and our lives seem deadly blank.

19   Lytton Strachey. Letter to Leonard Woolf, Nov. 26, 1906.

Two days after Thoby's death, Vanessa became engaged to Clive Bell. Strachey again reported the news to Woolf.

20   Photograph of Violet Dickinson.

21   Virginia Stephen. "Friendships Gallery." Typescript, with manuscript corrections in the author's and unidentified hands.

This was written as a tribute to her friend Violet Dickinson, with whom she traveled to Italy in the spring of 1904, and who nursed her through her second breakdown, after her father's death.

22   Photograph of 29 Fitzroy Square, London.

After Vanessa's marriage in 1907, Virginia and Adrian moved to Fitzroy Square, where they remained until 1911.

23   Vanessa Bell. Letter to her sister, Virginia Stephen, [April 11, 1908].

Saturday.

My Billy

. . . Are you enjoying life without me? I hope you feel the difference, or are you too much engrossed in me as a subject for your art to be able to think of me in the flesh? I am

reading your Life of Violet again & really find it very witty
& brilliant (what should I have said?) but I wonder more &
more how you ever dared to show it to her. It brings me
back to the atmosphere of rarified culture & free talk which
is so congenial to me & is a solace from talk of Julian and
the winter of '81.

You can imagine that I play the part of the proud mother
even less well than I did that of the engaged young lady,
but on the whole the baby provides a very useful topic of
conversation on which we can all discourse for some time
without fear of running on to Art or Religion. I look at
these surroundings & feel thankful that he is still too young
to know the difference between ugliness & beauty & in
fact rather enjoys the many shining brass knots which meet
the eye everywhere, but it will be awful when we have to
educate his taste & point out how hopelessly wrong every-
thing here is. Poor little wretch, he's been howling all day
& so perhaps he knows more than we think. I'm going to
begin his one bottle now & shall soon increase it to two I
think for really my milk shows signs of being too little. . . .

Julian Bell, Vanessa's first child, was born February 4, 1908.

24   Francis Dodd. *Adeline Virginia Woolf*, 1908. Reproduction
     of a portrait in the National Portrait Gallery.

25   Aeschylus. *Agamemnon*. Manuscript of Virginia Woolf's
     English translation, with her marginal notes on the Greek
     text.

Virginia was, unlike her brothers, educated at home, where
she had free run of her father's extensive library. She also
had a tutor for Greek. For this translation of Aeschylus's
Agamemnon, Virginia mounted the original printed Greek
to face her manuscript translation into English. Leonard
Woolf believed "the translation was made, i.e., dictated, by
Janet Case and that it must be before 1912." In the early

It was probably in the summer of 1908 that Lytton Strachey
made his famous breakthrough in the conversational decencies of
the Stephen sisters, enlarging the frankness of subject matter
for which Bloomsbury was famous or notorious. As recounted by
Virginia:

*It was a spring evening [in Gordon Square]. Vanessa and I were
sitting in the drawing room. The drawing room had greatly
changed its character since 1904. The Sargent-Furse age was over.
The age of Augustus John was dawning. His Pyramus filled one
entire wall. The Watts portraits of my father and my mother
were hung downstairs if they were hung at all. Clive had hidden
all the match boxes because their blue and yellow swore with
the prevailing colour scheme. At any moment Clive might come in
and he and I should begin to argue – amicably, impersonally
at first; soon we should be hurling abuse at each other and pacing
up and down the room. Vanessa sat silent and I did something
mysterious with her needle or her scissors. I talked egotistically,
excitedly, about my own affairs no doubt. Suddenly the door
opened and the long and sinister figure of Mr Lytton Strachey
stood on the threshold. He pointed his finger at a stain on
Vanessa's white dress.*

"Semen?" he said.

*Can one really say it? I thought & we burst out laughing. With
that one word all barriers of reticence and reserve went down. A
flood of the sacred fluid seemed to overwhelm us. Sex permeated
our conversation. The word bugger was never far from our lips.
We discussed copulation with the same excitement and openness
that we had discussed the nature of good. It is strange to think
how reticent, how reserved we had been and for how long.*

(Quoted in Quentin Bell, *Virginia Woolf: A Biography*, I:124)

years of the new century, Janet Case succeeded Clara Pater, Walter Pater's sister, as Virginia's Greek instructor. Their relationship developed into friendship; Case was instrumental in rousing Virginia's latent feminism into active advocacy.

26 Adrian Stephen. *The "Dreadnought" Hoax*. London: Hogarth Press, 1936.

This is Adrian Stephen's account of the visit on February 10, 1910, to the British Navy's latest ship, H.M.S. *Dreadnought*, of a group disguised as the Emperor of Abyssinia and his entourage. The group, under the leadership of Horace Cole, included five others, among them Virginia Woolf in blackface, moustache, and beard. Their object, in Quentin Bell's words, was "to hoodwink the British Navy, to penetrate its security and to enjoy a conducted tour of the flagship of the Home Fleet, the most formidable, the most modern and the most secret man o' war then afloat."

27 Dorothea Jane Stephen. Letter to Virginia Stephen, March 3, 1910.

Not everyone appreciated the humor of the "Dreadnought hoax." Virginia received a letter from one of her Stephen cousins criticizing her participation and suggesting her behavior was owing to her lack of religious beliefs.

28 Virginia Woolf. "The Voyage Out." Holograph.

The Voyage Out, Virginia's first novel, was begun in 1908 and was finished in March 1913; it was offered to the publishing firm of her half brother, Gerald Duckworth, who accepted it for publication. It remained unpublished, however, for two years, years during which Virginia suffered and recovered from a breakdown; the months following publication were "the most violent and raving . . . of her madness" (Quentin Bell).

This draft of *The Voyage Out* is from ca. 1910 with revisions from 1912. Its title at this stage was "Melymbrosia." Louise DeSalvo edited the manuscripts of *Melymbrosia* for publication by the Library in 1982.

29 Vanessa Bell. Letter to her sister, Virginia Stephen, [July 5, 1910].

Virginia spent most of the summer of 1910 at Jean Thomas's nursing home at Twickenham on the advice of her physician, Dr. George Savage. One of Vanessa's letters to Virginia relates a visit to Ottoline and Philip Morrell and their conversation about love affairs, including that of her brother Adrian with Duncan Grant:

Tuesday.

My Billy.

I saw Savage this morning & he said that I might write to you once or twice a week. Apparently you have been making yourself too charming & witty a companion to Miss Thomas – I couldnt make out some obscure reference to a musical evening with the nurses [?] – but anyhow Savage said that neither your sleep nor your head were yet recovered & that you werent to see anyone at present. Do restrain your gifts & dont waste them on your asile [?]. I had not seen S. before & so have heard nothing more from him about your state. Probably he said much more to you than he did to me for I had only a short interview. The only other thing he said was that you certainly would quite recover if you carried out his orders.

We have been gloomy since you departed, with no gaieties beyond an evening at Figaro where, for a wonder, there was practically nobody we knew & one at Ottoline's. Clive, Adrian & I went there, & Duncan & Henry Lamb also came in for a short time. It was dull while they were there but after they had gone Clive managed to stir up that effete couple to some kind of life by talking about love & jealousy.

Ottoline has evidently had some love affairs of a serious kind since she married but told me in an undertone that it was impossible to talk about them before Philip. I have asked her to come to tea tomorrow & if I succeed in getting more out of her I will tell you. But I'm afraid she wont confide in me. Philip said he was never jealous of her but obviously is. Adrian described anonymously his affair with Duncan – they talked quite freely of passion "inverted" – & displayed a coolness & want of either passionate or calm affection which was curiously in accord with this [?] analysis. He is almost too odd. We have not seen much of him, as I assume that he spends most of his time with Duncan. . . .

30   E. M. Forster. *Howards End*. London: E. Arnold, 1910.

Forster's fourth novel, which he considered his best, appeared in 1910.

31   Edmund Gosse. Letter to Edward Marsh, Dec. 27, 1910.

Although the reviews of *Howards End* were largely favorable and solidified Forster's reputation as a novelist, not everyone was won over by it. Edward Marsh sent a copy of the novel to Edmund Gosse, one of England's leading men of letters, who found it "as a whole . . . sensational and dirty and affected."

32   Sydney Waterlow. Diary, Dec. 8, 1910. Holograph.

Sydney Waterlow was a Cambridge friend of Clive Bell's and in his diary reports on a visit to the Bells:

Dined with the Clive Bells: what a relief & change! No one else but Virginia S. We had talk that begins to be really intimate. Vanessa very amusing on paederasty among their circle. I realized for the first time the difference between her & Virginia: Vanessa icy, cynical, artistic; Virginia much more emotional, & interested in life rather than beauty.

"In or about December, 1910, human character changed"
– *Virginia Woolf*

And now I will hazard a second assertion, which is more disputable perhaps, to the effect that in or about December, 1910, human character changed.

I am not saying that one went out, as one might into a garden, and there saw that a rose had flowered, or that a hen had laid an egg. The change was not sudden and definite like that. But a change there was, nevertheless; and, since one must be arbitrary, let us date it about the year 1910. The first signs of it are recorded in the books of Samuel Butler, in The Way of All Flesh *in particular; the plays of Bernard Shaw continue to record it. In life one can see the change, if I may use a homely illustration, in the character of one's cook. The Victorian cook lived like a leviathan in the lower depths, formidable, silent, obscure, inscrutable; the Georgian cook is a creature of sunshine and fresh air; in and out of the drawing-room, now to borrow the* Daily Herald, *now to ask advice about a hat. Do you ask for more solemn instances of the power of the human race to change? Read the* Agamemnon, *and see whether, in process of time, your sympathies are not almost entirely with Clytemnestra. Or consider the married life of the Carlyles and bewail the waste, the futility, for him and for her, of the horrible domestic tradition which made it seemly for a woman of genius to spend her time chasing beetles, scouring sauce-pans, instead of writing books. All human relations have shifted – those between masters and servants, husbands and wives, parents and children. And when human relations change there is at the same time a change in religion, conduct, politics, and literature. Let us agree to place one of these changes about the year 1910.*

(Virginia Woolf, "Mr. Bennett and Mrs. Brown")

1910 was the year of the first Post-Impressionist exhibition at the Grafton Gallery, curated by Roger Fry, and featuring Manet, Cézanne, Gauguin, Van Gogh, and Matisse. The exhibition was controversial, the public was outraged. Writing in the *Morning Post*, Robert Ross saw the exhibition as an effort to "destroy the whole fabric of European painting."

Rupert Brooke in costume as
Comus, Cambridge, July 1908
(item 33)

33 **Photograph of Rupert Brooke in his costume for the title role in Milton's *Comus*, performed at Cambridge in July 1908.**

Brooke came into Virginia's orbit through the Strachey/ Cambridge connection. In August 1911, Virginia paid a visit to Brooke's home, the Old Vicarage, Grantchester. One evening Brooke suggested, "Let's go swimming quite naked" in the Granta, and they did. "[I]t was an act worthy of Vanessa, a gesture of emancipation. If Adrian is to be trusted, she was a little vexed that it did not create more of a sensation amongst her friends" (Quentin Bell).

34 **Lytton Strachey. Letter to Leonard Woolf, Nov. 16, 1907.**

Strachey reports meeting Rupert Brooke at Cambridge – "poetical and pseudo-beautiful, with red hair and complexion complete" – and discusses Brooke's likely election to the "Apostles."

35 **Gwen Raverat. Letter to Virginia Woolf, April 22, 1925.**

Gwen Darwin married Jacques Raverat in 1911. The Raverats were painters and members of the Neo-Pagans, a group of largely Cambridge-connected figures, chief among whom was Rupert Brooke. Although Brooke had been an intimate friend of James Strachey, Lytton's younger brother, there was no love lost between Bloomsbury and Brooke, as Raverat recalled in this letter.

36 **Virginia Stephen. Letter to Violet Dickinson, [June 4, 1912].**

Leonard Woolf returned from Ceylon in 1911 and immediately rejoined his Cambridge friends. Over the years a number of people, including Lytton Strachey and Sidney Waterlow, had unsuccessfully proposed marriage to Virginia. (Strachey's proposal was actually accepted, but both he and Virginia realized almost immediately the improbability of their union.)

My Violet,

*I've got a confession to make. I'm going to marry Leonard
Wo[o]lf. He's a penniless Jew. I'm more happy than anyone
ever said was possible – but I insist upon your liking him
too. May we both come on Tuesday? Would you rather I
come alone? He was a great friend of Thobys, went out to
India – came back last summer when I saw him & he's
been living here since the winter.*

*You have always been such a splendid & delightful creature,
whom I've loved ever since I was a mere chit, that I couldn't
bear it if you disapproved of my husband. We've been talking a great deal about you. I tell him you [are] 6 ft 8: & that
you love me.*

*My novels just upon finished. L. thinks my writing the best
part of me. We're going to work very hard. Is this too
incoherent? The one thing that must be made plain is my
intense feeling of affection for you. How I've bothered you –
& what a lot you've always given me.*

Yr. Sp[arroy].

37 **Leonard and Virginia Woolf in 1912, the year of their
marriage. Frontispiece of: Leonard Woolf.** *Beginning Again.*
**London: Hogarth Press, 1964. Presentation copy, inscribed,
from the author to Lola L. Szladits.**

38 **Roger Fry. Letter to Leonard Woolf, [1912], sending
congratulations to Woolf on his engagement.**

39 **Sydney Waterlow. Diary, July 1912. Holograph.**

Virginia Stephen married Leonard Woolf on August 10, 1912.

Waterlow, who had proposed marriage to Virginia in 1911
(perhaps his entry for November 29, 1911, "Spoke to
Virginia," alludes to the occasion), pasted into his diary a
newspaper notice of the Woolfs' August wedding.

WOOLF : STEPHEN.—On Saturday, the 10th Aug., at the St. Pancras Register Office, LEONARD SIDNEY WOOLF, son of the late Sidney Woolf, Q.C., and of Mrs. Sidney Woolf, of Lexham, Colinette-road, Putney, to VIRGINIA STEPHEN, daughter of the late Sir Leslie Stephen, K.C.B.

40 Desmond MacCarthy. [Sir Sydney Waterlow]. Holograph draft of obituary notice for the London *Times*, [1944].

41 "April 15, 1913. Dear Henry James. . . ." [London? 1913].

Henry James was an old friend of the Stephens, and in his later years James got to know many of the younger generation of writers, including those gathered under the label of Bloomsbury.

This printed letter sending greetings to Henry James on his 70th birthday was signed by 242 "friends and admirers" – "a roll call of splendor in the annals of the arts, politics and the social life of the time" (Leon Edel) – including Sir James M. Barrie, Arnold Bennett, Bernard Shaw, and Virginia Woolf. The signers subscribed five pounds each to pay for a Charles II porringer and dish for the author of *The Golden Bowl* and for a portrait of James to be painted by John Singer Sargent (who refused to accept a fee for the work).

42 John Singer Sargent. *Henry James*. Reproduction of a portrait now in the National Portrait Gallery.

Sargent's portrait was completed late in 1913. While on display at the Royal Academy in May of the following year, it was attacked with a meat cleaver by a militant suffragette as a protest on behalf of "political freedom" for women.

43 Jean Thomas. Letter to Violet Dickinson, Sept. 14, [1913].

Virginia's third breakdown, in 1913, involved a suicide attempt. In a letter to Violet Dickinson, Thomas, who was in charge of a mental hospital at Twickenham, attributed Virginia's state to panic while correcting the proofs of *The Voyage Out*.

44 **Desmond MacCarthy. Letter to Virginia Woolf, Jan. 8, 1914, recounting a visit to Henry James.**

45 **Cambridge Conversazione Society. Invitation to dine at the Connaught Rooms, London, on June 26, 1914.**

46 **Leonard Woolf. *The Wise Virgins: A Story of Words, Opinions and a Few Emotions*. London: E. Arnold, 1914.**

Leonard inscribed this copy of his novel for his wife on October 7, 1914.

47 **Photograph of 17 The Green, Richmond, Surrey.**

The Woolfs moved into the second-floor apartment at 17 The Green, Richmond – a short train ride from London – on October 16, 1914, while Virginia was recovering from her 1913 breakdown.

48 **Virginia Woolf. Diary, Jan. 25, 1915. Holograph.**

Virginia began what may ultimately be recognized as her masterpiece, one of the world's greatest diaries, on Friday, January 1, 1915. The first volume breaks off after the entry for February 15, about six weeks before the publication of her first novel, and is not taken up again until August 3, 1917. In the interval, Virginia suffered her most severe period of madness to date.

49 **Virginia Woolf. "The Voyage Out." Later typescript draft, with the author's ms. corrections.**

50 **Virginia Woolf. *The Voyage Out*. London: Duckworth, 1915.**

51   Photograph of Hogarth House, Richmond, Surrey.

The Woolfs moved into Hogarth House in March 1915 at a very difficult time: Virginia had entered a severe stage in her illness and for the first nine months of her residence required constant attendance.

52   Vanessa Bell. Letter to her sister, Virginia Woolf, May 10, [1916].

This letter touches on two topics, mobilization of civilians in World War I, and the design of a cloak for Virginia. Most of Bloomsbury was pacifist. Clothing was always a worry for Virginia.

May 10

My Billy,

I'm afraid I have been a long time writing about your cloak but as no doubt you have heard we have had rather an agitating time with the tribunals as both Duncan & Bunny [David Garnett] were refused any exemption. The tribunal consisted of perfectly bovine country bumpkins whose skulls couldnt be penetrated at all. They would hardly listen to anything & one felt at once that it was quite hopeless. Probably you'll have heard all about it from Adrian or someone so I wont go over it all again. Now we have to wait for the appeal but I havent much hope of that being any better.

It is rather difficult to design a cloak as I have no fashion plates here. I imagine the fashion now is to have it rather straight down to a very low belt & then rather wide on these [?] kind of lines but I dont suppose that is what you want. Havent you an old cloak that Joy could follow the general lines of? Perhaps that old white one with black lines? which was very pretty. I think it would be easier to do that than follow a vague sketch. . . .

My plans are rather vague until I know what happens at
the appeal. What are you doing? Are you back at Hogarth?
Do write & tell me all the gossip you can. I suppose every
[one] we know will soon be either in prison or the army. Will
Leonard be a C.O.? Please write soon.

Leonard, who suffered from a trembling of the hands, was
rejected for military service by the Army Medical Board.

53 Virginia Woolf. *Two Stories*, written and printed by
Virginia Woolf and L. S. Woolf. Richmond: Hogarth Press,
1917.

In her January 25, 1915, diary entry Virginia recorded her
and Leonard's decision to buy a printing press. The press
was ordered in March 1917 and delivered the following
month. They named their publishing venture the Hogarth
Press after their Richmond residence. Vanessa Bell designed
their logo, the wolf's head, a pun on the proprietors' name.
Vanessa also designed dust jackets for Virginia's books.

The first Hogarth publication, *Two Stories*, appeared in
1917 in an edition of 150 copies and contained "The Mark on
the Wall" by Virginia and "Three Jews" by Leonard Woolf.
The authors themselves printed the book on the hand press;
the four woodcut illustrations were by Dora Carrington.

54 Virginia Woolf. Letter to her sister, Vanessa Bell, May 22,
[1917].

Hogarth

May 22nd

. . . We've been so absorbed in printing that I am about as
much of a farmyard sheep dog as you are. I can hardly tear
myself away to go to London, or see anyone. We have just
started printing Leonards story; I haven't produced mine
yet, but there's nothing in writing compared with printing.
I want your advice about covers.

*We've got about 60 orders already, which shows a trusting
spirit, especially as most of them come from old ladies &
poets in the North, recommended by Bob Trevelyan whom
we've never heard of. Not one of our intimates has yet
bought a copy (this arrow is not aimed at you.)*

*However, I did rouse myself to go & see Ott[oline Morrell].
I was so much overcome by her beauty that I really felt
as if I'd suddenly got into the sea, & heard the mermaids
fluting on their rocks. How it was done I cant think; but she
had red-gold hair in masses, cheeks as soft as cushions
with a lovely deep crimson on the crest of them, & a body
really shaped more after my notion of a mermaid than I've
ever seen; not a wrinkle or blemish, swelling, but smooth.*

*Our conversation was rather on those lines, so I'm not
surprised that I made a good impression. She didn't seem
so much of a fool as I'd been led to think; she was quite
shrewd, though vapid in the intervals. I begged her to revive
Bedford Sq[ua]re & the salon, which she said she would, if
anyone missed her. Then came protestations, invitations –
in fact I dont see how we can get out of going there, though
Leonard says he wont, & I know it will be a disillusionment.
However, my tack is to tell her she is nothing but an illusion,
which is true, & then perhaps she'll live up to it. She was
full of your praises. "That exquisite head, on that lovely
body – a Demeter – promising loaves and legs of mutton for
us, and such sympathy, more feeling for others now. I did
so enjoy my time at Wissett." . . .*

55 Duncan Grant. *Vanessa Bell,* ca. 1916–18. Reproductions
of two portraits in the National Portrait Gallery.

56 Duncan Grant. "The Hat Shop," *Original Woodcuts by
Various Artists*. London: Omega Workshops Ltd., 1918.
No. 48 of 75 copies printed. E. McKnight Kauffer's copy,
with his autograph. Miriam and Ira D. Wallach Division
of Art, Prints and Photographs.

The Omega Workshops were founded in 1913 by Roger Fry at 33 Fitzroy Square. Their purpose was, like that of the Arts and Crafts movement, to integrate art into life through well-designed household articles. The contributing artists were influenced by the Post-Impressionists.

57   Katherine Mansfield. Letter to Virginia Woolf, [ca. Aug. 23, 1917].

The New Zealand short story writer Katherine Mansfield wrote to Virginia after a visit to Asheham, commenting on the similarity of their aims in writing, and the forthcoming Hogarth Press edition of her story *Prelude*.

We have got the same job, Virginia & it is really very curious & thrilling that we should both, quite apart from each other, be after so very nearly the same thing. We are you know: there's no denying it.

58   Katherine Mansfield. *Prelude*. Richmond: Hogarth Press, [1918]. One of 300 copies printed.

This copy of Mansfield's *Prelude*, the third publication of the Hogarth Press, is in its original lapis lazuli paper covers, with the line block design by J. D. Fergusson. Fergusson's design had been chosen by the author but was later dropped because Virginia disliked it.

59   Lytton Strachey. *Eminent Victorians: Cardinal Manning, Florence Nightingale, Dr. Arnold, General Gordon*. London: Chatto & Windus, 1918. From the library of Wallace Brockway.

Strachey's iconoclastic essays in biographical revisionism were an immediate success and revamped the writing of biography.

Hagiography was out.

60   Portrait photograph (reproduction) of Lytton Strachey.

61   Virginia Woolf. *Kew Gardens*. Decorated by Vanessa Bell. [London]: Hogarth Press, [1927]. 3rd edition. Two copies; no. 131 of 500 copies printed, signed by the author and the artist; no. 178 of 500 copies printed.

Kew Gardens, Virginia's third book, appeared on the same day that the Press issued T. S. Eliot's *Poems* and John Middleton Murry's *The Critic in Judgement*. A favorable review in *The Times Literary Supplement* ensured the book's success and marked the turning of the Press from an avocation to a business.

62   Virginia Woolf. [*Night and Day*. Chapters 11–17] "Dreams & Realities." Holograph draft, dated Oct. 6, 1916–Jan. 5, 1917.

A fragment of the draft of *Night and Day*, here given the working title "Dreams & Realities."

63   Virginia Woolf. *Night and Day*. London: Duckworth, [1919].

Virginia's second novel is dedicated "To Vanessa Bell but, looking for a phrase, I found none to stand beside your name."

64   Virginia Woolf. Postcard portrait, possibly issued for publicity purposes by George H. Doran Company, the American publisher of *The Voyage Out* and *Night and Day*.

65   John Maynard Keynes. *The Economic Consequences of the Peace*. London: Macmillan, 1919. David Garnett's copy, with his bookplate. Rare Books and Manuscripts Division.

Keynes, an important figure in Bloomsbury, whose economic theories were later to gain widespread acceptance.

represented the British Treasury at the Paris Peace Conference following World War I. In disagreement with the actions at Versailles in redrawing Europe's borders and imposing reparations, Keynes resigned from the Treasury to write this highly controversial attack on the Versailles Treaty. He was a revered *eminence* to the otherwise critical Bloomsberries.

66   Virginia Woolf. *Monday or Tuesday*. With woodcuts by Vanessa Bell. Richmond: Published by Leonard & Virginia Woolf at the Hogarth Press, 1921. One of 1,000 copies printed.

Monday or Tuesday includes "The Mark on the Wall," which appeared in the first publication of the Hogarth Press. The volume is open to the story "A Society," the only story of Virginia's that alludes to the "Dreadnought hoax." It is illustrated with one of Vanessa's woodcuts.

67   Virginia Woolf. "A Society." Typescript of story, with the author's ms. revisions.

68   Lytton Strachey. *Queen Victoria*. London: Chatto & Windus, 1921.

Strachey dedicated his biography of Queen Victoria to Virginia Woolf. The biography took a more sympathetic view of the sovereign than one might have anticipated from the author of *Eminent Victorians*.

69   Max Beerbohm. "Mr. Lytton Strachey, trying to see her with Lord Melbourne's eyes," in his: *A Survey*. London: W. Heinemann, 1921. Carl Van Vechten copy, with his bookplate.

70   F. M. Dostoevsky. *Stavrogin's Confession and The Plan of the Life of a Great Sinner*. With introductory and

explanatory notes. Translated by S. S. Koteliansky and Virginia Woolf. Richmond: Published by Leonard & Virginia Woolf at the Hogarth Press, 1922.

S. S. Koteliansky provided the translation from the Russian, which Virginia then improved.

71   Virginia Woolf. Diary, Jan. 26, 1920. Holograph.

Virginia records the conception of the yet-to-be-named *Jacob's Room* and comments on the "immense possibilities in the form" she would use, her own adaptation of the "stream of consciousness" technique also used by James Joyce and Dorothy Richardson.

. . . I see immense possibilities in the form I hit upon more or less by chance 2 weeks ago. I suppose the danger is the damned egotistical self; which ruins Joyce & [Dorothy] Richardson to my mind: is one pliant & rich enough to provide a wall for the book from oneself without its becoming, as in Joyce & Richardson, narrowing & restricting? My hope is that I've learnt my business sufficiently now to provide all sorts of entertainments. . . .

72   Virginia Woolf. "Jacob's Room." Holograph in 3 parts, dated April 15, 1920–March 12, 1922.

Virginia's note on the first page of the manuscript reads:

Reflections upon beginning a work of fiction to be called, perhaps, Jacobs Room. Thursday, April 15th 1920.

I think the main point is that it should be free.
Yet what about form?
Let us suppose that the Room will hold it together.
Intensity of life compared with immobility.
Experiences.
To change style at will.

Self-portrait, from
Twelve Original Woodcuts
by Roger Fry *(1922)*
(item 74)

73 Virginia Woolf. *Jacob's Room*. Richmond: Published by Leonard & Virginia Woolf at the Hogarth Press, 1922.

Virginia's third novel was published by the Hogarth Press with a press run of about 1,200 copies. The Press henceforth was to be Virginia's sole British publisher.

Jacob's Room, signalling Virginia Woolf's departure from the conventional realistic novel, is her first novel to employ the "stream of consciousness" technique: in a series of interior monologues by various characters, Woolf creates a rounded portrait of Jacob. The novel is an elegy for the author's brother, Thoby Stephen, who died in 1906.

74 Roger Fry. Self-portrait in *Twelve Original Woodcuts by Roger Fry*. Richmond: Printed and Published by Leonard & Virginia Woolf at the Hogarth Press, 1922. 3rd impression. Miriam and Ira D. Wallach Division of Art, Prints and Photographs.

75 David Garnett. *Lady into Fox*. Illustrated with wood engravings by R. A. Garnett. London: Chatto & Windus, 1922. Presentation copy, inscribed, from the author to Mina Kirstein Curtiss.

David Garnett, known to his friends as "Bunny," was the son of Edward and Constance Garnett and partner with Francis Birrell in the bookselling venture of Birrell & Garnett. His first book, *Lady into Fox*, winner of the 1923 Hawthornden Prize, was dedicated to Duncan Grant, father of Angelica Bell, who later became Mrs. David Garnett.

76 Desmond MacCarthy. *Criticism*. London: Putnam, [1932]. No. 17 of 100 copies signed by the author.

Desmond MacCarthy was the Cambridge man whom everyone in Bloomsbury expected to write a masterpiece; to Virginia he was "the most gifted of us all." An important drama critic, he also served as literary editor of the *New*

Statesman and for many years as the leading book reviewer for the London *Sunday Times*. But he never produced the great work that his friends felt was in him.

77   *Eliot Fellowship Fund.* **[n.p.], 1922. Printed circular requesting subscriptions to a special fellowship fund for T. S. Eliot. With a printed postscript modifying the terms of Eliot's possible use of the fund.**

In 1922, Richard Aldington, Lady Ottoline Morrell, and Virginia Woolf proposed the establishment of the Eliot Fellowship Fund to enable T. S. Eliot to give up his position as a bank employee and devote himself to writing. Eliot was uncomfortable with the idea.

This copy of the circular was sent by Virginia to Lytton Strachey on December 3, 1922. "Here at last," she wrote, "is the letter you have been anxiously waiting. It is worth keeping as a specimen of English." The "specimen of English" provided by the circular was that of its author, Lady Ottoline Morrell.

78   **Lytton Strachey. "The Lytton Strachey Donation." Holograph, unsigned, dated "Dec. 1922."**

In response to the circular soliciting funds for Eliot, Strachey drew up this mock proposal for the dispersion of £20,000 from his royalties.

79   **T. S. Eliot. Letter to Virginia Woolf, Dec. 4, 1922.**

Much to Eliot's irritation, the *Liverpool Daily Post and Mercury* reported the attempt to raise money for Eliot. After commenting on the matter, Eliot offers his initial reaction to *Jacob's Room*.

80   **Photograph of Lytton Strachey, Virginia Woolf, and Goldsworthy ("Goldie") Lowes Dickinson, ca. 1922, at Garsington.**

Dickinson was a fellow of King's College, Cambridge, and later the subject of a biography by E. M. Forster.

81   **Katherine Mansfield. *The Garden Party and Other Stories*. London: Constable, [1922].**

Published the year before her early death from consumption, *The Garden Party* is Mansfield's best volume of short stories. While novelist Dorothy Richardson is often mentioned in relation to Woolf, because both were pioneers in the use of the "stream of consciousness" method, it was Mansfield whom Virginia felt was her true competition (and vice versa).

82   **Virginia Woolf. Diary, Jan. 16, 1923. Holograph.**

Following Katherine Mansfield's death on January 9, 1923, Virginia reflected on their relationship in her diary.

83   **Howard Coster. *Vita Sackville-West*, 1934. Reproduction of a portrait in the National Portrait Gallery.**

84   **Virginia Woolf. Diary, Dec. 15, 1922. Holograph.**

Virginia met Vita Sackville-West (Mrs. Harold Nicolson), who was to play such a prominent part in her life, for the first time at a dinner party given by Clive Bell. In her diary for Friday, December 15, Virginia records the meeting:

. . . This is partly the result of dining to meet the lovely gifted aristocratic Sackville West last night at Clive's. Not much to my severer taste – florid, moustached, parakeet coloured, with all the supple ease of the aristocracy, but not the wit of the artist. She writes 15 pages a day – has finished another book – publishes with Heinemanns – knows everyone – But could I ever know her? I am to dine there on Tuesday. . . .

85   Portrait photograph of Harold Nicolson.

86   Virginia Woolf. Letter to Barbara Bagenal, July 8, [1923].

. . . I assure you the Press is worse than 6 children at breast simultaneously. Consider the Sow. She shows no embarrassment. But Leonard & I live apart – he in the basement, I in the printing room. We meet only at meals, often so cross that we cant speak, & generally dirty. His triumphs always coincide with my disasters. When one's up, the other's down. Then you & the Sow say that maternity is worse! I have just finished setting up the whole of Mr Eliots poem with my own hands. . . .

Mr. Eliot's poem is, of course, *The Waste Land*, for which Virginia herself set type for the Hogarth Press edition.

87   T. S. Eliot. "The Waste Land." Typescript, with the author's and Ezra Pound's ms. revisions.

88   Snapshot of T. S. Eliot outside Faber & Gwyer (later Faber & Faber), publishers.

This photograph came to the Berg Collection with Frank Morley's papers. Morley, brother of Christopher Morley, was to become a co-director with Eliot of Faber & Faber.

89   T. S. Eliot. *The Waste Land*. Richmond, Surrey: Printed and published by Leonard and Virginia Woolf at the Hogarth Press, 1923. Proof copy of the first English edition, with the author's ms. corrections.

90   T. S. Eliot. *The Waste Land*. Richmond, Surrey: Printed and published by Leonard and Virginia Woolf at the Hogarth Press, 1923. One of about 460 copies printed. Presentation copy, inscribed, from the author to John Middleton Murry, Katherine Mansfield's husband; with three ms. corrections by Eliot in the volume.

91 T. S. Eliot. Letter to Virginia Woolf, [Sept. 14, 1923].

Eliot enumerates the typographical errors he failed to correct when he read the proofs of *The Waste Land* and mentions his efforts to do so after publication.

92 Richard Kennedy. Floor plan of the Hogarth Press, 52 Tavistock Square, London. Original pen-and-ink drawing. Lent by Mrs. Olive Kennedy through the kind offices of the Whittington Press.

From 1924 to 1939, the Woolfs rented the basement, where the Press was located, and the top two floors at 52 Tavistock Square, not far from Gordon Square. Virginia had a studio at the back of the basement where she did most of her writing, including much of *Mrs. Dalloway*, *To the Lighthouse*, and *Orlando*. Kennedy's drawing depicts Virginia at work at the back amid the Press's activity.

93 Virginia Woolf. "Mr. Bennett & Mrs. Brown." Holograph corrections dated May 1, 1924, in a notebook also containing fragments of *Mrs. Dalloway*.

94 Virginia Woolf. *Mr. Bennett and Mrs. Brown*. London: Published by Leonard and Virginia Woolf at the Hogarth Press, 1924. (The Hogarth Essays, 1.) One of 1,000 copies printed; cover design by Vanessa Bell.

When read to the Heretics at Cambridge on May 18, 1924, the lecture was entitled "Character in Modern Fiction" and was "as near as she came to an aesthetic manifesto" (Quentin Bell). In the lecture, she criticized Arnold Bennett, John Galsworthy, and H. G. Wells, the leading realistic novelists of the day.

95 Vita Sackville-West. "Seducers in Ecuador." Holograph.

In her diary for September 15, 1924, Virginia wrote that Vita "left with us a story which really interests me rather. I see my own face in it, its true. But she has shed the old verbiage, & come to terms with some sort of glimmer of art; so I think: & indeed, I rather marvel at her skill, & sensibility; for is she not mother, wife, great lady, hostess, as well as scribbling?" Vita dedicated the book to Virginia.

96   Vita Sackville-West. *Seducers in Ecuador*. London: Published by Leonard and Virginia Woolf at the Hogarth Press, 1924. One of 1,500 copies printed.

97   Virginia Woolf. Letter to Vita Sackville-West, [Sept. 15, 1924].

Monday

My dear Vita,

I like the story very very much – in fact, I began reading it after you left, was interrupted by Clive, went out for a walk, thinking of it all the time, & came back & finished it, being full of a particular kind of interest which I daresay has something to do with its being the sort of thing I should like to write myself. I don't know whether this fact should make you discount my praises, but I'm certain that you have done something much more interesting (to me at least) than you've yet done. It is not, of course, altogether thrust through; I think it could be tightened up, & aimed straighter, but there is nothing to spoil it in this. I like its texture – the sense of all the fine things you have dropped in to it, so that it is full of beauty in itself when nothing is happening – nevertheless such interesting things do happen, so suddenly – barely too; & I like its obscurity so that we can play about with it – interpret it different ways, & the beauty & fantasticallity of the details – the butterflies & the negress, for instance. This is all quite sincere, though not well expressed.

I am very glad that we are going to publish it, & extremely proud & indeed touched, with my childlike dazzled affection

for you, that you should dedicate it to me. We sent it to the
printer this morning. . . .

The Hogarth Press would eventually publish over a dozen
volumes by Vita Sackville-West.

98 Two portrait drawings (reproductions) of Vita Sackville-
West.

99 E. O. Hoppé. Portrait photograph (reproduction) of Vita
Sackville-West.

100 Vita Sackville-West. *Sissinghurst*. London: Printed by
hand by Leonard & Virginia Woolf and published at the
Hogarth Press, 1931. No. 7 of 500 copies printed;
signed by the author.

This poem about the author's home and beloved garden is
dedicated to Virginia Woolf.

101 E. M. Forster. *A Passage to India*. London: E. Arnold, 1924.

This was the last novel Forster published in his lifetime.
His homosexual novel, *Maurice*, written in 1913 and 1914,
was published posthumously in 1971.

102 Reproduction of a 1921 photograph of E. M. Forster in
Indian court costume taken when he served as private
secretary to the Maharajah of Dewas State Senior.

103 Virginia Woolf. *The Common Reader*. London: Published
by Leonard & Virginia Woolf at the Hogarth Press, 1925.
Cover design by Vanessa Bell.

104 Virginia Woolf. *The Common Reader*. New York: Harcourt,
Brace, [1925]. 1st American edition.

The essays in *The Common Reader*, which Virginia dedicated

to Lytton Strachey, touch on aspects of English literature from Chaucer and the Elizabethan dramatists, through Daniel Defoe and Joseph Conrad to the state of contemporary fiction as represented by Wells, Bennett, and Galsworthy. This first series of *The Common Reader* also contains essays on the three most distinguished women novelists of the 19th century: Jane Austen, Charlotte Brontë, and George Eliot.

105　Virginia Woolf. ["Modern Fiction"] "Modern novels (Joyce)." Holograph notebook.

Virginia was the exact contemporary of James Joyce: both were born in 1882 and died in 1941.

106　Leonard Woolf. *Fear and Politics: A Debate at the Zoo*. London: Published by Leonard and Virginia Woolf at the Hogarth Press, 1925. (The Hogarth Essays, 7.) Cover design by Vanessa Bell.

107　"Famous Dancer's Wedding." *The Daily Mirror*, London, Aug. 5, 1925. Rare Books and Manuscripts Division.

This newspaper clipping reports John Maynard Keynes's marriage to ballerina Lydia Lopokova.

108　John Maynard Keynes. Letter to Virginia Woolf, June 8, 1928.

Keynes invites the Woolfs to join him at a ballet performance in which his wife will dance in the presence of the King and Queen.

109　Virginia Woolf. [*Mrs. Dalloway*] "The Prime Minister." Holograph and typescript, with the author's ms. corrections.

<u>Mr. Dalloway.</u>   <u>Nov: 9th 1922</u>

So far Mrs D in Bond Street &
the P.M. are written.

    too jerky & minute. Some
general style must be found, or ones
attention is too broken.

    Suppose the idea of the book is
the contrast between life & death.

All inner feelings to be lit up.
The two minds. Mrs D. & Septimus.
And the design is something like
this —
      Mrs. D. ~~end~~ comes on alone.
(as in first chapter)
    We then go on to a general
statement, introducing Septimus.
    They are linked together by
the aeroplane.
    We then return to Mrs D.
alone in her drawing room.
& settle into her.

First page of Virginia
Woolf's holograph notes for
Mrs. Dalloway *(item III)*

The manuscript of *Mrs. Dalloway* is in the British Library, but the Berg archive contains much holograph material relating to the novel.

110 Virginia Woolf. "Mrs Dalloway in Bond Street." In: *The Dial*, **75, no. 1 (July 1923).**

The short story "Mrs Dalloway in Bond Street" was written as, but subsequently rejected for, the first chapter of *Mrs. Dalloway*, and is closely related to the novel.

111 Virginia Woolf. [*Mrs. Dalloway*]. Holograph notes, dated Nov. 9, 1922–Aug. 2, 1923.

112 Virginia Woolf. *Mrs. Dalloway*. **London: Published by Leonard & Virginia Woolf at the Hogarth Press, 1925.**

The novel was published on May 14, 1925, in a first printing of about 2,000 copies. The Dalloways had made a brief appearance as characters in Virginia's first novel, *The Voyage Out*.

113 Photograph of Lord North Street, Westminster, London.

This is one of the streets near Westminster Abbey on which the Dalloways' house may have been located.

114 Virginia Woolf. *Mrs. Dalloway*. **Introduction by Virginia Woolf. New York: Modern Library, [1928].**

In her introduction to the Modern Library edition of *Mrs. Dalloway*, the author revealed "that in the first version Septimus, who later is intended to be her double, had no existence; and that Mrs. Dalloway was originally to kill herself, or perhaps merely to die at the end of the party."

115 E. M. Forster. ["The Early Novels of Virginia Woolf"] "Virginia Woolf." Holograph essay.

This essay first appeared in 1926 in *The Criterion*, and was collected in *Abinger Harvest* in 1936. Of *Mrs. Dalloway* Forster wrote, "It is perhaps her masterpiece. . . ." This was written prior to the publication of *To the Lighthouse*, which Forster was ultimately to consider her best work.

116 E. M. Forster. *Abinger Harvest*. London: E. Arnold, [1946]. Carl Van Vechten's copy, with his bookplate.

117 Howard Coster. *E. M. Forster*, 1938. Reproduction of a portrait in the National Portrait Gallery.

118 Virginia Woolf. "To the Lighthouse." Holograph in 3 parts, dated Monks House and 52 Tavistock Square, Aug. 6, 1925–March 16, 1927.

119 Virginia Woolf. *To the Lighthouse*. London: Published by Leonard & Virginia Woolf at the Hogarth Press, 1927.

Mr. and Mrs. Ramsay were based on Virginia's parents. The setting of the novel is the Hebrides, but clearly evokes memories of the Cornwall in which the Stephen family spent its summer vacations.

120 Photographs of Talland House, St. Ives, Cornwall, the summer retreat of the Stephen family and site of *To the Lighthouse* (although in the novel tactfully relocated to the Hebrides). Gift of Glyn and Cathy Roberts.

121 Vanessa Bell. Letter to her sister, Virginia Woolf, May 11, [1927].

Villa Corsica
May 11

My Billy,

. . . it seemed to me that in the first part of the book you have given a portrait of mother which is more like her to me

First page of the manuscript of
To the Lighthouse *(item 118)*

than anything I could ever have conceived of as possible.
It is almost painful to have her so raised from the dead. You
have made one feel the extraordinary beauty of her charac-
ter, which must be the most difficult thing in the world to
do. It was like meeting her again with oneself grown up &
on equal terms & it seems to me, the most astonishing feat
of creation to have been able to see her in such a way.
You have given father too I think as clearly, but perhaps I
may be wrong, that isnt quite so difficult. There is more to
catch hold of. Still it seems to me to be the only thing about
him which ever gave a true idea. So you see as far as por-
trait painting goes you seem to me to be a supreme artist &
it is so shattering to find oneself face to face with those two
people again that I can hardly consider anything else. In
fact for the last two days I have hardly been able to attend
to daily life. . . .

122   Julia Margaret Cameron. Portrait photograph of Julia
      Prinsep Jackson Stephen at Freshwater in 1874. Gift of
      Hamill and Barker in memory of Dr. John D. Gordan.

123   Leonard Woolf. "Foreword" to Mitchell A. Leaska's
      Virginia Woolf's Lighthouse. Typescript, with the author's
      ms. corrections. Gift of Mitchell A. Leaska.

124   E. M. Forster. *Aspects of the Novel*. London: E. Arnold,
      1927. Presentation copy, inscribed, from the author to
      Norman Matson, "10-11-27."

Aspects of the Novel consists of the Clark Lectures delivered
by Forster at Cambridge in the spring of 1927.

125   Virginia Woolf. Checkbook and two cancelled checks.
      Anonymous loan (promised gift).

Virginia had a checking account at the Russell Square
Branch of the Midland Bank. The check dated November 30,
1927, is made out to Leonard Woolf in the amount of one

*Virginia's mother, Julia
Prinsep Jackson Stephen, at
Freshwater in 1874, in a
portrait photograph by Julia
Margaret Cameron, Mrs.
Stephen's aunt (item 122)*

pound: the check dated January 2, 1936, is made out to the Principal, Brighton Technical College. The checkbook, covering the period December 9, 1930–February 11, 1931, includes a stub dated January 2, 1931, recording a birthday gift of five guineas to her nephew, Julian Bell.

126   Clive Bell. "Civilization: An Essay." Holograph, with the author's ms. revisions.

Bell dedicated *Civilization* to Virginia Woolf, whose private opinion of it was that Bell "has great fun in the opening chapters but in the end it turns out that Civilisation is a lunch party at no. 50 Gordon Square" (Quentin Bell), the Bells' residence.

Bell also contributed the concept of "significant form" to aesthetic theory.

127   Clive Bell. *Civilization: An Essay*. London: Chatto & Windus, 1928.

128   Virginia Woolf. Letter to Vita Sackville-West, Oct. 9, [1927].

Virginia apprises Vita of the birth of *Orlando*, a work that Vita's son Nigel called Virginia's "most elaborate love-letter."

Yesterday morning I was in despair. . . . I couldn't screw a word from me; & at last dropped my head in my hands: dipped my pen in the ink, & wrote these words, as if automatically, on a clean sheet: Orlando: A Biography. No sooner had I done this than my body was flooded with rapture & my brain with ideas. I wrote rapidly till 12. Then I did an hour to Romance. So every morning I am going to write fiction (my own fiction) till 12; & Romance till 1. But listen; suppose Orlando turns out to be Vita; & its all about you & the lusts of your flesh & the lure of your mind (heart you have none, who go gallivanting down the lanes with Campbell). . . .

The identification of Vita with Orlando was evident to the public in the dedication of the book to her and by the fact that Vita posed for several of the portraits of Orlando.

129 Virginia Woolf. Letter to Vita Sackville-West, Oct. 13 [i.e., 14, 1927].

. . . The poor Wolves have been having colds in the head. Mine I caught in a dentists waiting room: but thats neither here nor there. The point is the incident symbolises our friendship. Now think carefully what I mean by that. There's a dying hue over it: it shows the hectic dolphin colours of decay. Never do I leave you without thinking, its for the last time. And the truth is, we gain as much as we lose by this. Since I am always certain you'll be off & on with another next Thursday week (you say so yourself, bad creature, at the end of your last letter, which is where the viper carries its sting) since all our intercourse is tinged with this melan-[c]holy on my part & desire to be white nosed & so keep you half an instant longer, perhaps, as I say we gain in intensity what we lack in the sober comfortable virtues of a prolonged & safe & respectable & chaste & cold blooded friendship.

I am writing at great speed. For the third time I begin a sentence, The truth is — The truth is I'm so engulfed in Orlando I can think of nothing else. It has ousted romance, psychology & the rest of that odious book completely. To-morrow I begin the chapter which describes Violet [Trefusis] & you meeting on the ice. The whole thing has to be gone into thoroughly. I am swarming with ideas. Do give me some inkling what sort of quarrels you had. Also, for what particular quality did she first choose you? Look here: I must come down & see you, if only to choose some pictures. I want one of a young Sackville (male) temp. James 1st: another of a young Sackville (female) temp. George 3rd.

Please lend yourself to my schemes. It will be a little book, about 30,000 words at most, & at my present rate which is feverish (I think of nothing but you all day long, in different guises, & Violet & the ice & Elizabeth & George the 3rd) I shall have done it by Christmas. Thats to say, if we dont go to Russia: Do you want me to go to Russia? We're been asked to go there, free, by the Government, to celebrate the anniversary of Revolution for one month. Dont you think one should take the chance, buy furs, & risk the cold? Tell me what you think. I must settle by Tuesday.

Orlando will be a little book, with pictures & a map or two. I make it up in bed at night, as I walk the streets, every-where. I want to see you in the lamplight, in your emeralds. In fact, I have never more wanted to see you than I do now – just to sit & look at you, & get you to talk, & then rapidly & secretly, correct certain doubtful points. About your teeth now, & your temper. Is it true you grind your teeth at night? Is it true you love giving pain? What & when was your moment of greatest disillusionment? And then you say there's a squalid reason, the flux I suppose, & you cant come! Still my nose was red, so I forgive you. . . .

130 Virginia Woolf. *Orlando: A Biography*. New York: Crosby Gaige, 1928. 861 copies printed; no. 777 of 800 offered for sale.

131 Virginia Woolf. *Orlando: A Biography*. London: Published by Leonard and Virginia Woolf at the Hogarth Press, 1928.

132 Harlingue-Viollet. Photograph (reproduction) of Virginia Woolf.

133 Victoria, Lady Sackville. Letter to F. N. Doubleday, Sept. 22, 1930.

Portrait of Vita Sackville-West
as Orlando, from the Hogarth
Press edition of the novel
(item 131)

Vita Sackville-West's mother expresses her distress over the publication of *Orlando*.

134   Vita Sackville-West. Diary of a journey to France with Virginia Woolf in 1928. Holograph, dated Sept. 24–30, 1928.

Virginia and Vita spent a week traveling alone together in France shortly before the publication of *Orlando*.

135   Radclyffe Hall. Letter to Gerard Hopkins, Aug. 15, 1928.

Radclyffe Hall's autobiographical novel about lesbianism, *The Well of Loneliness*, was banned in Britain by the Home Secretary, William Joynson-Hicks ("Jix"), on the grounds of obscenity. It became a literary cause célèbre in which Virginia Woolf and E. M. Forster became involved. In this letter to Hopkins, Hall reviews the book's reception, singling out for particular attack a review by Leonard Woolf in *The Nation*.

136   Howard Coster. *Radclyffe Hall*, 1932. Reproduction of a portrait in the National Portrait Gallery.

137   Virginia Woolf. Letter to Vita Sackville-West, Aug. 30, 1928.

In response to the threat to suppress *The Well of Loneliness*, a group of prominent writers undertook to support the book's right to be published. E. M. Forster, a lifelong defender of freedom of speech, was among those organizing petitions, and Virginia was among the signers. As Virginia writes to Vita, a major snag arose when Radclyffe Hall said she would accept their support only if they put forth her view – which Virginia and Forster were unwilling to do – that *The Well of Loneliness* was a great literary work.

. . . For many days I have been so disjected by society that writing has been only a dream – something another woman

did once. What has caused this irruption I scarcely know –
largely your friend Radclyffe Hall (she is now docked of her
Miss owing to her proclivities). They banned her book; & so
Leonard & Morgan Forster began to get up a protest, & soon
we were telegraphing & interviewing & collecting signatures
– not yours, for your proclivities are too well known. In
the midst of this, Morgan goes to see Radclyffe in her tower
in Kensington, with her love [Una, Lady Troubridge]: &
Radclyffe scolds him like a fishwife, & says that she wont
have any letter written about her book unless it mentions the
fact that it is a work of artistic merit – even genius. And no
one has read her book; or can read it: & now we have to
explain this to all the great signed names – Arnold Bennett
& so on. So our ardour in the cause of freedom of speech
gradually cools, & instead of offering to reprint the master-
piece, we are already beginning to wish it unwritten.

138   E. M. Forster. Letter to Arnold Bennett, Aug. 31, 1928.

Forster informs Bennett of Hall's raising difficulties on the
part of her defenders. Virginia and Forster were prepared to
testify at the trial, but the presiding magistrate refused to
allow discussion of the novel's merit and declared the book
obscene.

139   Virginia Woolf. *A Room of One's Own*. New York:
The Fountain Press; London: The Hogarth Press, 1929.
492 copies printed; no. 431 of 450 offered for sale.
Signed by the author on the half title. Elizabeth R. and
Morton Freund bookplate.

"This essay is based upon two papers read to the Arts
Society at Newnham and the ODTAA at Girton in October
1928." Newnham and Girton were the only two Cambridge
colleges to admit women; the name of the ODTAA Society
stood for "one damn thing after another." One of Virginia's
arguments in this feminist essay is that until women have
the privacy of "a room of one's own" and the independence

provided by an income of 500 pounds a year, they will not be able to take their rightful place in the literary scene. She also argues for the androgyny of the artist.

140   Harcourt, Brace and Company. Letter, signed Donald Brace, to Leonard Woolf, Aug. 1, 1929, relating to a limited edition of *A Room of One's Own*.

141   Virginia Woolf. "Dorothy Wordsworth." Extracted from *New York Herald Tribune Books*, Oct. 27, 1929.

142   London Artists' Association. *Recent Paintings by Vanessa Bell, with a Foreword by Virginia Woolf*. February 4th to March 8th 1930. [London, 1930]. Two of about 500 copies printed.

143   Virginia Woolf. *On Being Ill*. [London]: Printed and Published by Leonard & Virginia Woolf at the Hogarth Press, 1930. No. 75 of 250 numbered and signed copies. Rare Books and Manuscripts Division.

144   Humbert Wolfe. ["Bloomsberries"]. Holograph draft of unfinished poem.

Wolfe was an extraordinarily popular poet in the late 1920s and early 1930s, one of whose prose pieces was published by the Hogarth Press. At his death in 1940, Virginia recorded in her diary that he had told her that he was often asked if she was his wife.

145   Virginia Woolf. *Street Haunting*. San Francisco: Westgate Press, 1930. No. 301 of 500 copies printed by the Grabhorn Press; signed by the author. Rare Books and Manuscripts Division.

146   Photograph of Virginia Woolf and Dame Ethel Smyth.

147 Virginia Woolf. Diary, Aug. 25, 1930. Holograph.

In February 1930, Virginia met the composer Ethel Smyth, a feminist who was moved to meet Virginia after reading *A Room of One's Own*. Smyth was much older, deaf, and a demanding friend. In her diary for August 25, 1930, Virginia recounts Dame Ethel's visit to Rodmell.

148 Photograph of Virginia Woolf at age 49.

149 Virginia Woolf. *Beau Brummell*. New York: Rimington & Hooper, 1930. 550 copies printed; no. 328 of 500 copies offered for sale. Designed by W. A. Dwiggins and printed by The Printing House of William Edwin Rudge; signed by the author.

150 Virginia Woolf. [*The Waves*] "The Moths? or the life of anybody; life in general or Moments of being or The waves." Holograph drafts, dated July 2, 1929–July 1, 1931.

151 Virginia Woolf. *The Waves*. London: Published by Leonard and Virginia Woolf at the Hogarth Press, 1931. Elizabeth R. and Morton Freund bookplate.

152 Lytton Strachey. "Acrostiche Invertie." Holograph sonnet sent to Roger Senhouse.

153 Lytton Strachey. *Portraits in Miniature and Other Essays*. London: Chatto & Windus, 1931. Dedication copy, signed by the author and presented to Max Beerbohm; with the latter's inscription after Strachey's death in 1932: "And, Brother, for all time Hail and Farewell!"

In a letter to Virginia Woolf, Beerbohm had written that "Lytton Strachey's prose is, *on the whole*, the finest English prose that has been written."

To
MAX BEERBOHM
WITH GRATITUDE
AND ADMIRATION

from
Lytton Strachey

" And, Brother, for all time
Hail and Farewell! "

Max 1932

154   Max Beerbohm. "Lytton Strachey." Holograph of the Rede Lecture for 1943.

155   Max Beerbohm. *Lytton Strachey*. New York: Alfred A. Knopf, 1943. Carl Van Vechten bookplate.

156   Dora Carrington. Letter to Roger Senhouse, [1932].

Lytton Strachey died on January 21, 1932. During his last years he had been looked after by the artist Dora Carrington and her husband, Ralph Partridge. Carrington was in love with Strachey, and she committed suicide on March 11, less than two months after Lytton's death.

157   Virginia Woolf. ["The London Scene"] "The Docks of London," *Good Housekeeping*, December 1931. Corrected page proofs.

Virginia loved London and loved to walk about it. For the British *Good Housekeeping* she wrote a series of articles on "The London Scene," beginning with "The Docks of London."

158   Virginia Woolf. *A Letter to a Young Poet*. London: Published by Leonard & Virginia Woolf at the Hogarth Press, 1932. (The Hogarth Letters, 8.)

159   John Lehmann. Letter to Julian Bell, March 10, 1931.

Early in 1931, John Lehmann, a college friend of Julian Bell's, was hired as trainee manager of the Hogarth Press, a position he gave up after eighteen months. He eventually became a partner in the press in 1938, buying out Virginia's share. (Lehmann is the poet to whom Virginia's *A Letter to a Young Poet* is addressed.)

160   Virginia Woolf. "How should one read a book?" Holograph draft of essay.

This was one of the essays included in *The Common Reader: Second Series*.

161   Virginia Woolf. *The Common Reader: Second Series*. London: Published by Leonard & Virginia Woolf at the Hogarth Press, 1932. Presentation copy, inscribed, from Leonard Woolf to the Berg Collection. Dust jacket designed by Vanessa Bell.

162   Virginia Woolf. [*Flush*] "The life, character & opinions of Flush the Spaniel." Holograph fragment of opening chapter, dated July 21, 1931.

Virginia liked to alternate a serious novel with a lighter and less demanding work such as *Orlando* or *Flush*.

163   Virginia Woolf. *Flush: A Biography*. London: Published by Leonard and Virginia Woolf at the Hogarth Press, 1933.

Flush records the life of Robert and Elizabeth Barrett Browning as seen through the eyes of Elizabeth's spaniel, Flush. Vanessa Bell provided four illustrations for *Flush*.

164   Elizabeth Barrett Browning. [*Flush*]. Original pen-and-ink sketch inside the front cover of a holograph notebook of working drafts of poems.

165   Harcourt, Brace and Company. Letter, signed Donald C. Brace, to Virginia Woolf, Aug. 21, 1933, informing her that *Flush* has been accepted as a Book-of-the-Month Club selection.

166   Virginia Woolf. "Freshwater: A Comedy." Typescript, with the author's ms. corrections, [1923].

Virginia wrote two versions of this play about her great-aunt, the photographer Julia Margaret Cameron. This typescript is of the earlier version, ca. 1923. The play received one performance only (in the later version) in 1935 at 8 Fitzroy Street. The cast was:

C. H. H. Cameron	Leonard Woolf
Mrs. Julia Cameron	Vanessa Bell
G. F. Watts	Duncan Grant
Ellen Terry	Angelica Bell
Lord Tennyson	Julian Bell
Mr. Craig	Ann Stephen
Mary (a maid)	Eve Younger
Queen Victoria	Eve Younger

167 **"Angelica Garnett in the role of Ellen Terry." Frontispiece of: Virginia Woolf.** *Freshwater: A Comedy.* **Edited and with a preface by Lucio P. Ruotolo. Illustrated by Loretta Trezzo. New York: Harcourt Brace Jovanovich, [1976].**

Angelica Garnett is the daughter of Vanessa Bell and Duncan Grant. In addition to playing Ellen Terry in *Freshwater*, she posed for the illustration of "The Russian Princess as a Child" in *Orlando*.

168 **Virginia Woolf.** *Walter Sickert: A Conversation.* **London: Published by Leonard and Virginia Woolf at the Hogarth Press, 1934. Cover design by Vanessa Bell.**

This essay on one of Britain's major twentieth-century artists first appeared in *The Yale Review* (September 1934) under the title "A Conversation About Art." It remained uncollected until the posthumous volume *The Captain's Death Bed and Other Essays* (1950).

169 **Wyndham Lewis.** *Men Without Art.* **London: Cassell, [1934]. Carl Van Vechten bookplate.**

While Virginia was now the foremost English woman novelist of her generation and her books were selling very well, she and her Bloomsbury colleagues were not without their detractors. Representative, perhaps, of the hostile critics are Wyndham Lewis and Frank Swinnerton, whose *Georgian Literary Scene*, critical of Bloomsbury, appeared in 1935.

Lewis's survey of contemporary fiction devotes chapters to Hemingway and Faulkner, Flaubert, James, and, of course, Virginia Woolf, whom he posits as representative of the feminine element in contemporary letters. His position, as might be expected, was openly hostile: "Mrs. Woolf is extremely insignificant . . . she is a purely feminist phenomenon . . . she is taken seriously by no one any longer today, except perhaps by Mr. and Mrs. Leavis. . . ."

170   Virginia Woolf. [*The Years*] "The Pargiters. A Novel-Essay based upon a paper read to the London/National Society for Women's Service." Holograph, dated Oct. 11, 1932–Nov. 15, 1934.

Other titles considered by Virginia in the course of writing *The Years* were: Time Passes; Here and Now; In the Flesh; The Dawn; Uncles and Aunts; Ordinary People; and Sons and Daughters. *The Pargiters: The Novel-Essay Portion of The Years* was edited by Mitchell A. Leaska and published by the Library in 1977.

171   Virginia Woolf. [*The Years*. London: Published by Leonard and Virginia Woolf at the Hogarth Press, 1937]. Galley proofs, incomplete, with the author's ms. corrections.

172   Virginia Woolf. *The Years*. London: Published by Leonard and Virginia Woolf at the Hogarth Press, 1937. Dust jacket designed by Vanessa Bell.

173   Virginia Woolf. *Années*. Traduit de l'anglais par Germaine Delamain. Préface de René Lalou. Paris: Editions Stock, 1938.

The Years—174

encouraging ~~a~~ horse. ~~She almost expected him to make a cluck at the back of his throat. She felt the tension of his muscles,~~ as if he were ~~doing his best to help the engine on.~~ They slowed—they almost stopped. No, now they were on the crest of the hill. She had done it on top!

"Well done!" she exclaimed. He said nothing; but he was very proud, she knew.

"We couldn't have done that on the old car," she said.

"Ah, but it wasn't her fault!" said Cole.

He was a very humane man, she reflected; the kind of man she liked. ~~She relaxed now, for the road was clear ahead; she could look about her.~~

"~~So that house is let at last?~~" she said as they passed ~~a low~~ grey stone house ~~behind a gate.~~ Ill-kept bushes grew right up to the front door. ~~For fifty years an~~ eccentric lady ~~had~~ lived ~~there,~~ alone with peacocks and bloodhounds; ~~issuing out only at dusk and heavily veiled. But the postman was now delivering letters. A solicitor from York had taken it, Cole said, a man of the name of Rudge.~~ They ~~sped~~ on. Now the woods were on their right hand and the air came singing through them. ~~It sounded~~ like the sea, Kitty thought, looking as they passed, down a dark green drive patched with yellow sunlight. ~~They sped on.~~ Heaps of ruddy brown leaves lay by the roadside staining the puddles red.

"It's been raining?" she said. He nodded. ~~Spring comes very slowly, she thought; but when it came, it was real: it was spring truly.~~ They came out on the high ridge with the woods beneath, and there, in a clearing among the trees, ~~there was a green grey roof; a clock tower; and the spark of a glasshouse. It was the first sight of the Castle.~~ She always looked out for it and greeted it as if she were raising her hand to a friend. ~~Now~~ they were on their own land. Gate-posts were branded with their initials; their arms hung above the signboard of the inns; their crest was mounted over cottage doors. Cole looked at the clock.

"~~We shall do it under the three-quarters, m'lady,~~" ~~he said. He was still cautious; but there was triumph in his voice. The old car had never done it under the hour.~~ The needle leapt again.

Too fast, too fast! Kitty said to herself. But she liked the rush of the wind in her face. Now they reached the Lodge gate; Mrs Preedy was holding it open with a white-haired child on her arm. ~~Kitty nodded as they rushed past.~~ They swept round through the park. The deer looked up and hopped lightly away through the ferns. ~~There ahead of them was the old grey house.~~

"Two minutes under the three-quarters, m'lady,"

She felt the tension of his muscles.

On they swept past the where they had passed it.

mad

? Correct. see copy. was the grey tower of the Castle.

Now

Now here they were

The Years was the seventh of Virginia's books to be translated into French.

174   **Julian Bell. Letter to John Lehmann, Sept. 25, [1936].**

Vanessa Bell's son Julian. writing from China where he was teaching. speaks of Spain and the Spanish Civil War: "it seems the right place to be if one can get there."

175   *Julian Bell: Essays, Poems and Letters*. **Edited by Quentin Bell. With Contributions by J. M. Keynes, David Garnett, Charles Mauron, C. Day Lewis, and E. M. Forster. London: Hogarth Press, 1938.**

On July 18. 1937. while serving with the British Medical Unit in Spain during the Spanish Civil War. Julian Bell was killed at age twenty-nine by a bomb that hit the ambulance he was driving.

This collection of his essays. poems. and selections from his correspondence was published the year following his death. This copy belonged to the artist Su Hua Ling Chen. whom he met while teaching at Wuhan University. China. and with whom he had a love affair.

176   **Virginia Woolf. [*Three Guineas*]. Holograph and typescript, with the author's ms. corrections.**

177   **Virginia Woolf. *Three Guineas*. London: The Hogarth Press, 1938. Dust jacket designed by Vanessa Bell.**

Three Guineas was conceived as a sequel to *A Room of One's Own*. A summary of it was published in the *Atlantic Monthly* (May/June 1938) under the title "Women Must Weep – Or Unite Against War."

178   *Lady Ottoline's Album*. **New York: Knopf, 1976. General Research Division.**

This collection of "snapshots and portraits of her famous contemporaries (and of herself), photographed for the most part by Lady Ottoline Morrell" includes several pages on Virginia Woolf at Garsington Manor, Lady Ottoline's estate near Oxford.

179   **Lady Ottoline Morrell. "A Farewell Message." [n.p., 1938]. Sir Edward Marsh's copy.**

Lady Ottoline Violet Anne Cavendish-Bentinck Morrell died on April 21, 1938. Her husband, Philip Morrell, sent this farewell message to friends.

180   **Stephen Tennant. [Lady Ottoline Morrell]. Pen-and-ink and watercolor sketch.**

181   **Virginia Woolf. "[Lady] Ottoline Morrell." Typescript, with the author's and Leonard Woolf's ms. corrections.**

Virginia's obituary of Lady Ottoline appeared in the London *Times*, April 28, 1938.

182   **Gisèle Freund. Photograph (reproduction) of Leonard Woolf, ca. 1939.**

183   **Virginia Woolf. *Reviewing*. With a Note by Leonard Woolf. London: The Hogarth Press, 1939. (Hogarth Sixpenny Pamphlets, 4.)**

184   **Virginia Woolf. Letter to Su Hua Ling Chen, April 17, 1939.**

Virginia comments on the war, on the progress of her biography of Roger Fry, and on the imminent move from Tavistock Square to Mecklenburgh Square. The work of Su Hua Ling's that Woolf mentions is her autobiographical *Ancient Melodies*.

185   Virginia Woolf. "Roger Fry: A Biography." Typescript, fragment, with the author's ms. corrections, and Leonard Woolf's ms. identifying note.

186   Virginia Woolf. *Roger Fry: A Biography*. New York: Harcourt, Brace, [1940]. 1st American edition.

Virginia's biography of her friend, the art critic and painter Roger Fry, was to be the last book she saw through the press and her only true biography. The manuscript fragments of the book in the Berg Collection are intermingled with passages from her last novel, *Between the Acts*.

187   Vanessa Bell. Letter to her sister, Virginia Woolf, [March 13, 1940].

Virginia sent a copy of the manuscript of *Roger Fry* to Roger's sister Margery and to Vanessa.

Charleston – Wednesday – midnight.

Since Julian died I havent been able to think of Roger. Now you have brought him back to me. Although I cannot help crying I cant thank you enough. VB

188   Vanessa Bell. *Leonard Sidney Woolf*, 1940. Reproduction of a portrait in the National Portrait Gallery.

189   Virginia Woolf. "Between the Acts." Final typescript, with the author's ms. corrections and Leonard Woolf's editorial corrections and instructions to the printer.

190   John Lehmann. "Note on typescripts of 'Between the Acts.' . . ." Typescript, dated June 1974.

Lehmann authenticates the final typescript as the one Virginia gave him for a "casting vote" as to whether or not the novel was publishable.

Virginia Woolf
(item 201)

191 Virginia Woolf. *Between the Acts*. London: The Hogarth Press, 1941. Dust jacket designed by Vanessa Bell.

Between the Acts was published July 17, 1941.

192 Gisèle Freund. Photograph (reproduction) of Virginia Woolf, 1939.

193 Virginia Woolf. "Anon." Holograph and typescript fragments.

"Anon.," of which fragments exist in the Berg Collection, was incomplete at Woolf's death. It "was to be a kind of history of literature; it was to be written for Duncan [Grant] in order to explain to him what English Literature was about. The difficulty was, Virginia said, that she had reached a point at which she had to explain Shakespeare; his genius was universal and her book might therefore be rather long" (Quentin Bell).

194 Virginia Woolf. Letter to Ethel Smyth, Feb. 1, 1941.

Did I tell you I'm reading the whole of English literature through? By the time I've reached Shakespeare the bombs will be falling. So I've arranged a very nice last scene: reading Shakespeare, having forgotten my gas mask, I shall fade far away, & quite forget . . . They brought down a raider the other side of Lewes yesterday. I was cycling in to get our butter, but only heard a drone in the clouds. Thank God, as you would say, one's fathers left one a taste for reading! Instead of thinking, by May we shall be – whatever it may be: I think, only 3 months to read Ben Jonson, Milton, Donne, & all the rest. . . .

195 Virginia Woolf. Diary, March 24, 1941. Holograph.

Virginia made her last entry in her diary on March 24, 1941.

The concluding line reads: "L[eonard]. is doing the rhododendron:"

Virginia committed suicide by drowning on March 28, 1941, in the River Ouse.

She had a nose like the Duke of Wellington & great honest eyes. When we came in she was sitting perched on a 3 cornered chair with knitting in her hand. An arrow fastened her collar. And before 5 minutes had passed she had told us that two of her sons had been killed in the war. This, one felt, was to her credit. She then taught dress making. Everything in the room was red brown & glossy. Sitting there I tried to coin a few compliments. But they perished in the icy seas between us. And then there was nothing.

A curious sea side feeling in the air today. It reminds me of lodgings on a parade at Easton. Eugene leaning against the wind, nipped & silenced. All pulp removed. This windy corner. And Nessa is at Brighton & I am imagining how it wd be if we could infuse souls.

Octavia's story. Could I englobe it somehow? English youth in 1900. Two long letters from Shena & O. I cant tackle them, yet enjoy having them. L. is doing the rhododendrons.

*Virginia's final diary entry,
written March 24, 1941,
four days before her death
(item 195)*

SELECTED BIBLIOGRAPHY

Bell. Quentin. *Bloomsbury*. New York: Basic Books, [1969].

Bell. Quentin. *Virginia Woolf: A Biography*. New York: Harcourt Brace Jovanovich, 1972. 2 v. in 1.

Furbank. P. N. *E. M. Forster: A Life*. New York: Harcourt Brace Jovanovich, 1978.

Holroyd. Michael. *Lytton Strachey*. New York: Holt, Rinehart and Winston, [1968]. 2 v.

Kirkpatrick. B. J. *A Bibliography of Virginia Woolf*. 3rd ed. Oxford: Clarendon Press, 1980.

Leaska. Mitchell A. *The Novels of Virginia Woolf: From Beginning to End*. [New York]: John Jay Press, City University of New York, 1977.

Lehmann. John. *Virginia Woolf and Her World*. New York: Harcourt Brace Jovanovich, [1975].

Woolf. Virginia. *The Diary of Virginia Woolf*. Edited by Anne Olivier Bell; Introduction by Quentin Bell. New York: Harcourt Brace Jovanovich, 1977–[84]. 5 v.

Woolf, Virginia. *The Letters of Virginia Woolf.* Editor, Nigel
Nicolson; Assistant Editor, Joanne Trautmann. New York:
Harcourt Brace Jovanovich, [1975–80]. 6 v.

Woolmer, J. Howard. *A Checklist of the Hogarth Press,
1917–1946.* With a short history of the Press by Mary E.
Gaither. Revised and enlarged ed. Revere, Pa.: Woolmer/
Brotherson, 1986.

ILLUSTRATIONS

Other Titles of Interest from the Berg Collection

Charles Dickens 1812–1870: An Anthology from the Berg Collection

Dandies and Doughties: Writers in Britain 1890–1900

Edna St. Vincent Millay, 1892–1950

Love and Death

Pen and Brush: The Author as Artist

Perennials: A Fiftieth Anniversary Selection from the Berg Collection

W. H. Auden, 1907–1973

Walt Whitman: In Life or Death Forever

This edition of 1,000 copies was set in Bauer Bodoni and Univers Extended and printed by The Stinehour Press in Lunenburg, Vermont. The paper used is Mohawk Superfine, an acid-free, 200-year-life paper. This book was designed by Judith Hudson and edited by Barbara Bergeron at The New York Public Library.